D0463327

Steve Austin
The Story of the Wrestler They Call "Stone Cold"

Ric Flair
The Story of the Wrestler They Call "The Nature Boy"

Bill Goldberg

Bret Hart
The Story of the Wrestler They Call "The Hitman"

The Story of the Wrestler They Call "Hollywood" Hulk Hogan

Kevin Nash

Dallas Page
The Story of the Wrestler They Call "Diamond" Dallas Page

Pro Wrestling's Greatest Tag Teams

Pro Wrestling's Greatest Wars

Pro Wrestling's Most Punishing Finishing Moves

The Story of the Wrestler They Call "The Rock"

Randy Savage
The Story of the Wrestler They Call "Macho Man"

The Story of the Wrestler They Call "Sting"

The Story of the Wrestler They Call "The Undertaker"

Jesse Ventura
The Story of the Wrestler They Call "The Body"

The Women of Pro Wrestling

CHELSEA HOUSE PUBLISHERS

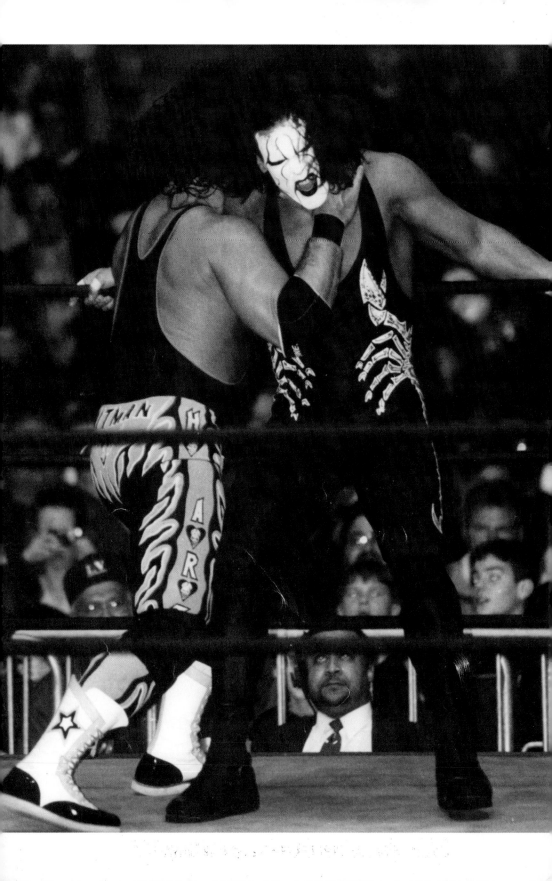

J
796.812
Ros
2001

Pro Wrestling's Greatest Wars

Dan Ross

Chelsea House Publishers
Philadelphia

WOODLAND PUBLIC LIBRARY

Produced by Choptank Syndicate, Inc.

Editor and Picture Researcher: Mary Hull
Design and Production: Lisa Hochstein

CHELSEA HOUSE PUBLISHERS

Editor in Chief: Stephen Reginald
Production Manager: Pamela Loos
Art Director: Sara Davis
Director of Photography: Judy L. Hasday
Managing Editor: James D. Gallagher
Senior Production Editor: J. Christopher Higgins
Project Editor: Anne Hill
Cover Illustrator: Keith Trego

Cover Photos: Jeff Eisenberg Sports Photography

© 2001 by Chelsea House Publishers,
a subsidiary of Haights Cross Communications. All rights reserved.
Printed and bound in the United States of America.

The Chelsea House World Wide Web site
address is http://www.chelseahouse.com

First Printing

1 3 5 7 9 8 6 4 2

Library of Congress Cataloging-in-Publication Data

Ross, Dan
        Pro Wrestling's greatest wars / by Dan Ross
            p. cm.—(Pro wrestling legends)
        Includes bibliographical references and index.
        Summary: Describes some of the more well-known feuds between various profes-
    sional wrestlers from the 1960s to the end of the twentieth century.
        ISBN 0-7910-5837-9 — ISBN 0-7910-5838-7 (pbk.)
        1. Wrestling—Juvenile literature. 2. Wrestlers—Biography—Juvenile literature
    [1. Wrestling.] I. Title. II. Series.

GV1195.3 R67 2000
796.812—dc21
                                                                    00-020732

Contents

1
A MATCH BECOMES A FEUD

One of the most telling scenes of the 1986 wrestling year wasn't played out in the ring or in the locker rooms, but in row 10 ringside at the Philadelphia Civic Center on a sultry summer night in August.

Outside the Civic Center, Philadelphia was suffering through a blistering heatwave. Inside, more than 8,000 fans were thrilling to a heatwave of a different type: another chapter in the long war between Rick Morton and Robert Gibson, known collectively as the Rock 'n' Roll Express, and Dennis Condrey and Bobby Eaton, the tag team known as the Midnight Express.

Fans had many reasons to hate the Midnight Express, not the least of which was the arrogant attitude of Condrey and Eaton. The Midnights' propensity for cheating was another. Most fans particularly hated Jim Cornette, the Midnights' loud, fast-talking manager. Yet there was one very simple reason National Wrestling Alliance (NWA) fans couldn't stand the sight of the Midnights: they were in a feud with the beloved Rock 'n' Roll Express.

The Rock 'n' Rolls were the polar opposites of the Midnights. Condrey and Eaton were mat wrestlers who liked to keep their matches on the ground, while Morton and Gibson were high-flyers. Condrey and Eaton dressed like tough guys

---

Determined to destroy one another, half brothers Undertaker and Kane waged one of the WWF's hottest feuds in the late 1990s.

from the mean streets, while Morton and Gibson dressed like teen rock idols. Condrey and Eaton would do anything to win, but Morton and Gibson believed in following the rulebook.

Unfortunately for the fans, Condrey and Eaton's "do anything to win" philosophy was succeeding for them. Although the Rock 'n' Rolls were the two-time former NWA World tag team champions, the Midnights had been wearing the belts for five months prior to this match, and had run up numerous victories over Morton and Gibson, thanks mostly to the ploys and interference of their manager.

On August 16, 1986, however, the good guys' fortunes took a turn for the better. Even Cornette's interference couldn't save the Midnights, who lost the World tag team belts to the Rock 'n' Rolls that night. Morton and Gibson were exultant. The fans' cheers were deafening. And in row 10 of the Civic Center, a middle-aged couple, both dressed in Rock 'n' Roll Express T-shirts, embraced and kissed as if they had just gotten married. That's how much the Rock 'n' Rolls' victory meant to them.

That's what feuds can do to wrestling fans.

Every sport has its rivalries: the New York Yankees vs. the Boston Red Sox in major league baseball, Duke vs. North Carolina in college basketball, or Florida vs. Florida State in college football. Pro wrestling has red-hot feuds, rivalries that have been super-charged with intensity and take on incredible lives of their own, resulting in the kinds of battles that can take your breath away.

Wrestling has rivalries, also. When Steve Austin wrestled Shawn Michaels at WrestleMania XIV, their match was definitely a rivalry, as each man wanted nothing more than to beat the other. Also on the card, Rocky Maivia wrestled Ken Shamrock in a rivalry of two tough, brutal competitors, But there was only one real feud on that WrestleMania XIV card: The Undertaker vs. Kane, his half brother, two men with long personal histories who were bent on not only beating, but destroying each other. That's when a rivalry becomes a feud—when merely winning isn't enough. A rivalry becomes a feud when the simple act of pinning one's opponent is only a prelude to the violence and mayhem to come.

Vince McMahon vs. Steve Austin was another hot feud. McMahon wanted to ruin Austin by

Known as the Rock 'n' Roll Express, good guys Rick Morton and Robert Gibson won the hearts of the fans when they wrestled the NWA tag team championship away from the rulebreaking Midnight Express during their 1986 feud.

running him out of wrestling forever. Austin, meanwhile, wanted to cripple McMahon, and, in the process, humiliate him and leave him penniless. Austin got his shots at McMahon in the ring, but winning didn't satisfy him. He wanted to rid the world of Vincent K. McMahon Jr.

Feuds are violent, heated, and dangerous. Matches and rivalries, however, bring fans out to the arenas and compel them to turn on WCW *Monday Nitro* and WWF *Monday Night Raw* each week. Feuds are capable of packing 70,000-seat arenas and creating millions of pay-per-view orders.

At its most powerful, a feud can change the very complexion of the sport. In 1998, Vince McMahon decided that Steve Austin's title reign would be a threat to the integrity of the WWF World title. Certainly, Austin vs. McMahon in the World Wrestling Federation (WWF) and the New World Order (NWO) vs. World Championship Wrestling (WCW) changed the sport in the 1990s, paving the way for an unprecedented explosion in wrestling's popularity.

In the early and mid-1990s, brothers Owen and Bret Hart waged a family feud to see who would claim the largest share of the WWF spotlight.

A feud can rock a family as much as it can change a sport. In the early- and mid-1990s, brothers Bret and Owen Hart shattered their families with a war that touched the hearts of almost every wrestling fan. Owen was tired of living in his brother's shadow. Their parents sobbed at ringside. Their brothers and sisters begged them to stop fighting. Yet Bret and Owen kept going after each other.

Owen was obsessed with destroying his brother, while Bret was determined to make sure that would never happen.

A feud can fascinate an entire state. In the 1980s, Texas wrestling fans were swept away by the feud between favorite sons the Von Erichs and the Fabulous Freebirds.

A feud can even cause divisions in ethnic groups, such as in 1972 when Pedro Morales, the hero of New York's large Hispanic population, battled Bruno Sammartino, the hero of New York's large Italian population, in a classic 75-minute match at Shea Stadium.

Feuds don't happen every day. Usually, there aren't more than a handful of real feuds in a given year. Something special, sometimes something seemingly insignificant to the casual observer, has to happen to turn a match or a rivalry into a feud.

In 1986, Hulk Hogan felt slighted when Paul Orndorff refused to take his phone call. That trivial incident triggered one of the most intense feuds in wrestling history; readers of *Pro Wrestling Illustrated* voted it feud of the year.

When that something special happens, sparks fly, people pay attention, and a federation's collective pulse rate accelerates. We realize that we're living in a special time, a dangerous time, a remarkable time when just about anything can happen. When two men who hate each other stop thinking rationally, and stop weighing the pros and cons of their actions, these men will do anything not just to win—but to destroy their hated foe. A match has become a feud. For the competitors involved, for the peers around them, and for the fans watching, the sport has taken on an incredible new life.

2

THE FEUDS OF
YESTERYEAR

As long as there have been wrestlers there have been feuds. Verifiable details of most of the true feuds of yesteryear are forever lost amidst rumor and misinformation. Indeed, for most of the 20th century, reporting and record-keeping for the sport of pro wrestling has been sketchy at best. Information about a few major feuds has survived, however, as testimony to their intensity.

Imagine two men wrestling nearly 100 matches over the course of an entire decade. That's a lot of hatred, and a lot of time spent trying to teach another man some manners. This was exactly what happened in the 1960s, however, as French-born scientific wrestler Edouard Carpentier would stop at nothing to teach "Killer" Kowalski a lesson in etiquette and respect.

"Wrestling's Longest Feud" is what *The Wrestler* magazine christened the war between Carpentier and Kowalski in 1964. "If I keep battling him long enough, maybe some of my manners will rub off on him," Carpentier said. "But I don't take any chances. You know what they say about a leopard never changing his spots."

The feud between Carpentier and Kowalski (who, at 6' 7" and 285 very mean pounds was one of wrestling's most dangerous men at that time) started when Carpentier, the most

Dick the Bruiser goes high in the air to pounce on a cringing Edouard Carpentier during their 1964 wrestling match.

In this 1935 photo, Ed "Strangler" Lewis is shown practicing the art that made him famous, with Ed Don George.

famous and decorated wrestler in France, was invited to wrestle in Canada. Kowalski, unlike most people, wasn't impressed by the gentlemanly Carpentier. "If that's the best the French can do, then they're in pretty bad shape," commented the surly Kowalski.

Shocked by his opponent's comments, Carpentier tried to mend fences with Kowalski, who merely insulted him further. Carpentier couldn't understand why a man he had never met would say such horrible things about him. The 5' 9", 220-pound Carpentier was angry and hungry for revenge.

Their first match in Montreal was a brutal battle. Kowalski was the meanest and most dangerous man Carpentier had ever faced. He tried to keep Carpentier off-balance with his acrobatic skills, but disaster struck when Kowalski stuck out his foot and injured Carpentier's kneecap. Somehow, though, Carpentier bravely battled back to score the pin.

Kowalski wasn't impressed. "He was carried off on a stretcher and didn't even hear the verdict that made him champion of Canada!" Kowalski gloated. "Some way for a guy to become a champ!"

Kowalski never forgave Carpentier, which was only fitting, since Carpentier never forgave Kowalski. Their feud raged across the United States and Canada. Through the years, they never once shook hands.

A few years prior to the Kowalski vs. Carpentier feud, "Cowboy" Bob Ellis and the Bruiser squared off in a feud that was all about sheer hatred. The feud started in 1959 in Indianapolis, Indiana, when the Bruiser made disparaging remarks about Ellis's blue jeans and five-gallon hat.

"You look like a cowboy the way I look like a ballet dancer," said Bruiser, who, at 6' 1" and 250 pounds, didn't look much like a ballet dancer at all. This was an insult, and Ellis got the message.

Then, when Ellis was signing autographs on his way to the ring, Bruiser grabbed some of the autographed pieces of paper and tore them to shreds. Ellis didn't fight back right away.

He waited until he and Bruiser were in the ring. When they got there, Bruiser slammed Ellis's head into a ringpost, opening up a thick gash. With blood pouring down his face, Ellis lost his composure and fought back like a wild man. When some of Ellis's friends intervened, Bruiser rushed back to the locker room.

Bruiser could run, but he couldn't hide. Ellis and Bruiser had countless battles in the ring, and each was more violent and bloody than the last. Their feud resulted in sell-out crowds throughout the Midwest and proved that even a mild-mannered man like Bob Ellis had a limit to which he could be pushed.

Another memorable feud was the 1971 series of battles between Fred Blassie and his former tag team partner, John Tolos. It all started

"Nature Boy" Buddy Rogers leaps to apply a head scissors to Paul Baillaegeon during a 1955 wrestling exhibition at Madison Square Garden.

"Cowboy" Bob Ellis claws the Masked Destroyer during a 1964 match in Los Angeles, refereed by "Smoky" Joe Wood.

when Blassie received an award as California's "Wrestler of the Year" and Tolos threw toxic Monsel's powder into Blassie's face. Blassie suffered severe corneal damage to his left eye, but that didn't stop him from seeking revenge.

Tolos, who had beaten Blassie for the Americas championship, believed he should have received the honor. In Blassie's mind, Tolos was angry because Blassie had broken up their tag team to become a singles wrestler. It didn't matter why these two men hated each other, though, they just did, with a passion that made their feud long, violent, and legendary.

On August 27, 1971, Blassie battled Tolos in front of 25,847 screaming fans at the Los Angeles Memorial Coliseum. When Blassie opened a deep cut on Tolos's head, Tolos was deemed unfit to continue. Blassie had finally won the war.

Throughout the 1970s, brothers Jack and Jerry Brisco had a long-running tag team and singles feud with the Funk family, Dory Jr. and his brother Terry. The fans were squarely on the side of the Briscos, but the Funks were tough and relentless. A match between Jack Brisco and Dory Funk Jr. in 1974 for the NWA World title was called "the greatest match in 30 years" by *The Wrestler* magazine. Brisco retained the title in a one-hour brawl, but ultimately lost the belt to Terry Funk on December 10, 1975.

Other notable feuds were not quite as heated, but still captured the fans' attention: Jim Londos vs. Ed "Strangler" Lewis in the 1930s; legendary grapplers Buddy Rogers and Lou Thesz in the 1950s and '60s; Dusty Rhodes vs. Harley Race for the NWA World title in the 1970s; Bruno Sammartino vs. Stan Stasiak, and later "Superstar" Billy Graham, for the WWF World title in the 1960s and '70s; Jimmy "Superfly" Snuka, an aerial acrobat like no other, vs. Bob Backlund for the WWF World title in the early 1980s; Snuka vs. "Magnificent" Don Muraco for the WWF Intercontinental title in the 1980s; and the tag team war in the late-1950s that pitted Carpentier and Antonino Rocca vs. Dick the Bruiser and Dr. Jerry Graham.

3

SINGLES FEUDS OF THE '80s AND '90s

From Bruno Sammartino vs. Larry Zbyszko in 1980 to Taz vs. Sabu in 1999, the last two decades of the 20th century were packed with long-running feuds that fascinated fans and helped drive pro wrestling to new heights of popularity.

BRUNO SAMMARTINO VS. LARRY ZBYSZKO

By 1980, Bruno Sammartino, who had dominated the WWF World title in the 1960s and '70s, was no longer World champion. The second of his two title reigns (totaling nearly 11 years) had ended in April 1977. But Bruno, known as "the Living Legend," was still a hero to millions, including, he thought, Larry Zbyszko.

As it turned out, Zbyszko was a bitter man. He was tired of being known as Sammartino's protégé. They had been friends for most of Larry's life. Bruno had given him his first big break by working out with him. Their seemingly unbreakable alliance broke when Zbyszko shockingly asked Sammartino for a match. Sammartino agreed.

When Zbyszko was flipped from the ring during the match, and Sammartino opened the ropes to allow him to reenter, Zbyszko grabbed a wooden chair from ringside and slammed it over Sammartino's head. The feud began, then gathered

---

Jerry "the King" Lawler flings an unknown substance into the eyes of WWF "King of the Ring" winner Bret Hart during a vicious match to determine who was the real king of the ring.

steam as Zbyszko started billing himself as "the New Living Legend."

Sammartino was both stunned and dismayed, but he was also angry at Zbyszko for betraying him. On August 9, 1980, Zbyszko and Sammartino had a showdown at Shea Stadium in New York. The gate receipts of $565,000 were, at the time, a North American record. The crowd of 40,671 watched Sammartino defeat Zbyszko in a cage match that hardly ended the feud. A year later, Sammartino retired, his feud with Zbyszko having never truly been settled.

HULK HOGAN VS. PAUL ORNDORFF

Hulk Hogan, the wildly popular WWF World champion, and Paul Orndorff, a slick blond with a history of rulebreaking, were actually friends in 1986. Most people thought this friendship couldn't last. After all, a year earlier Hogan and Mr. T had beaten Orndorff and Roddy Piper in the main event of WrestleMania I.

Behind the scenes, many wrestlers wondered whether Hogan was merely using Orndorff, keeping him on his good side to avoid having to face him in the ring. After a while, Orndorff started wondering the same thing, especially when Hogan refused to interrupt a training session to take a phone call from Orndorff, who became enraged as a result. The uneasy friendship between Orndorff and Hogan became a war when Orndorff turned against Hogan during a tag team match.

Now both men were enraged, Orndorff because he felt he had been slighted, Hogan because he felt he had been ambushed. On August 28, 1986, more than 74,080 fans, then an all-time wrestling attendance record, were on hand in Exhibition Stadium in Toronto to watch Hogan beat Orndorff. But that was only match one of a feud that burned throughout the year and turned Orndorff into wrestling's most hated man. They met 13 times in October alone, as Orndorff and Hogan concentrated all their energy on humiliating each other, with Hogan almost always emerging victorious.

HULK HOGAN VS. ANDRE THE GIANT

It was the feud that couldn't happen. They were two of the most popular wrestlers in history, loved by the fans and respected by the entire wrestling world.

In early 1987, Andre the Giant started to realize two things. First, he had been in the sport for three decades and, despite owning an incredible win-loss record, he had never been a World heavyweight champion. Second, his friend, WWF World champion Hulk Hogan, wasn't going to give him a title shot unless he demanded one.

So he demanded one. In an amazing change of personality, Andre shocked the wrestling world by hiring the notorious rule-breaker Bobby Heenan as his manager. Then he shocked Hogan when, in a face-to-face encounter, he ripped a prized chain from around Hogan's neck. Finally, Hogan had no choice but to grant Andre a title shot.

Their first showdown came at WrestleMania III on March 29, 1987, in Pontiac, Michigan. A crowd of 93,173 packed the Silverdome to watch the most anticipated match in wrestling history. Millions more watched on pay-per-view

Though Paul "Mr. Wonderful" Orndorff was once friends and tag team partners with Hulk Hogan, their relationship turned sour in 1986 and they began an energetic feud.

and closed-circuit television. In a spectacular match, Hogan defeated Andre after 12 minutes and one second of thrilling action.

Their feud didn't end there. It burned throughout the year and into the next, culminating in *The Main Event* on February 5, 1988, which marked wrestling's return to network prime-time television after an absence of 33 years. A month earlier, Andre had attacked Hogan at the contract signing. Now Andre ended Hogan's four-year WWF World title reign with a controversial pinfall victory. Immediately after winning, Andre gave the belt to his manager, Ted DiBiase.

For all intents and purposes, the Hogan vs. Andre feud ended at WrestleMania IV, when they battled to a double-disqualification in the second round of a tournament for the vacant World title. They would meet several more times in tag team matches, but their differences remained unsettled until Andre's death in 1993.

RANDY SAVAGE VS. RICK STEAMBOAT

In the mid-1980s, Randy "Macho Man" Savage was a man intent on keeping what was his. So when Rick Steamboat, one of the finest scientific wrestlers of all time, targeted his Intercontinental title Savage did as expected: he got meaner.

Their feud was not only one of the fiercest ever, it was also one of the finest ever between two outstanding wrestlers. It raged throughout the winter of 1986 and into 1987. As Steamboat's popularity grew, Savage got meaner and more hated. Finally, on March 29, 1987, Savage and Steamboat squared off at Wrestle-

Mania III before 93,173 fans at the Silverdome in Pontiac, Michigan.

The match was a classic. There were 19 two-counts, 11 by Steamboat, and most of the action in this fast-paced battle took place high above the mat and outside the ring. After 14 minutes and 35 seconds of non-stop action, Steamboat pinned Savage for the title.

Savage set his sights on regaining the belt, but Steamboat held off his violent and relentless attacks for two months. Their feud ended not with resolution, but with Steamboat shockingly losing the belt to the Honky Tonk Man. Savage turned his attention to the World title and ultimately became a fan favorite, while Steamboat faded out of the WWF picture.

HULK HOGAN VS. RANDY SAVAGE

They were rivals. Then they were friends. Then they were rivals again. When reviewing the great feuds of the 1980s, one stands out as the greatest of all: the Hulkster vs. the Macho Man.

Their friendship started at WrestleMania IV in 1988, when Hogan helped Savage win the WWF World title. The formation of the Megapowers—Hogan and Savage with the beautiful Elizabeth by their side—thrilled wrestling fans, but ultimately disappointed them.

Hogan and Savage were unbeatable, but their alliance was doomed to disaster. Their egos were too large. There was too much potential for jealousy. Hogan couldn't even look at Elizabeth without Savage getting insanely jealous. At the 1989 Royal Rumble, after Hogan clotheslined Savage to eliminate the Macho Man from the battle royal, Elizabeth tried to keep them together. She couldn't. A month

Whether wrestling Hulk Hogan, Ricky Steamboat, or Ric Flair, Randy "Macho Man" Savage was at the center of several prominent feuds in the 1980s and '90s.

later, during a nationally televised match pitting the Megapowers against Akeem and Big Bossman, Savage was thrown from the ring into Elizabeth, knocking her unconscious. Later, in the dressing room, Savage shoved Elizabeth, then attacked Hogan.

The fans hated Savage. Elizabeth didn't think much of him, either. At WrestleMania V, Hogan not only beat Savage for the World title, but ended up with Elizabeth, too. Savage enlisted the help of Sherri Martel, a former women's wrestling champion. At SummerSlam '89, Savage and Zeus lost to Hogan and Brutus Beefcake. A month later, Hogan held Savage as Elizabeth slapped him.

The feud was one-sided in Hogan's favor. Savage's victories were infrequent and were made possible only by Sherri's interference. Their rivalry died down, only to be rekindled seven years later in WCW, where Hogan once again held the edge over his longtime rival. Here, the Megapowers were briefly reunited.

BRET HART VS. OWEN HART

At the 1993 Survivor Series, Bret Hart teamed with his brothers, Owen, Keith, and Bruce, in a match against Shawn Michaels, the Black Knight, the Red Knight, and the Blue Knight. It was a dark time for the Hart family. Furious at an apparent slight by his brothers, Owen pushed Bret to the mat and screamed, "I don't need you!"

Owen's frustration with living in Bret's shadow boiled over that night. Bret had been one of the WWF's greatest superstars. Owen was struggling to work his way up the ladder. Stu Hart, their father, tried to reconcile Owen and Bret, but they had another misunderstanding at the 1994 Royal Rumble. Owen kicked Bret in the knee, then berated his brother. Their heartbreaking feud was underway.

At WrestleMania X, Owen spent most of a match against Bret trying to further damage Bret's injured left leg. It was a savage display of wrestling brutality, a shocking example of a man not caring about his own brother's welfare. At the 1994 King of the Ring, Bret's former partner, Jim Neidhart, helped Owen win the tournament.

"I can't believe what just happened," Bret said.

Owen and Bret met in a steel cage match at SummerSlam '94. Their feud intensified when Davey Boy Smith, their brother-in-law, interfered on Bret's behalf. The brother vs. brother feud included deception: at the 1994 Survivor Series, Owen convinced his mother, Helen, to throw in the towel for Bret during a submission match against Bob Backlund, costing Bret the WWF World title. For the next year, Bret's feud with Owen consumed most of his time and kept him from going after the belt.

This feud transcended the ring and split the family. Helen Hart, their mother, had many tearful, sleepless nights. Their father Stu Hart wondered what had gone wrong. Owen and Bret didn't reconcile until 1997, when they reformed the Hart Foundation. It was a tearful reunion.

Owen died in the ring in 1999. Sadly, his most memorable feud was the one against his beloved brother.

STEVE AUSTIN VS. BRET HART

The rivalry between Austin and Hart started at the 1996 Survivor Series when Hart, the WWF World champion, survived two "Stone Cold stunners" to defeat Austin by pinfall. Austin's cheating led to a victory in the January 1997 Royal Rumble, in which the last man he eliminated was Bret Hart, who was upset when the fans cheered Austin's victory.

Hart won the World title a month later in a four-way match that also included Austin, as well as Big Van Vader and The Undertaker. After he lost the title one day later to Sid Vicious, the fans started seeing Bret as a whiner. They turned against him completely at WrestleMania XIII. When he was introduced for his match against Austin, Bret heard boos for the first time in his career. Hart won the match with his sharpshooter leglock, then, with Austin lying unconscious on the mat, continued his assault. The boos got louder. Blood poured down Austin's face. Bret refused to break the hold. The boos became deafening.

Austin feuded with the entire Hart family— Bret, Owen, and Davey Boy Smith. As the cheers for Austin got louder, Hart's anger grew. One night, Shawn Michaels saved Austin from an attack by the Hart Foundation. There were more boos, and Bret felt betrayed by the fans.

"You U.S. fans don't respect me," Hart screamed angrily from the center of the ring. "Well, the fact is, I don't respect you. You don't deserve it."

Austin used a chair to injure Bret's knee and arm. The Canadian-born Bret was sidelined, and Austin laughed off the tirades that "Hitman" Hart continued from ringside.

Their feud was never settled, as Bret left the WWF in late 1997 and signed with WCW. Bret saw Austin as a symbol of all that has gone wrong with wrestling.

RIC FLAIR VS. RANDY SAVAGE

At the 1992 Royal Rumble, Flair eliminated Savage to win the vacant WWF World title, after which he announced that he'd had a relationship with Savage's wife Elizabeth several years earlier. Flair produced photos of the two of them together, and Savage was enraged. At WrestleMania XIII, Savage and Flair squared off in a violent match. Savage bloodied Flair to his liking, then scored the pin to win the World title. But Savage lost the title to Flair five months later and, by the end of the year, he and Elizabeth were divorced.

Their feud remained dormant until 1995, when Savage entered WCW and met up with his old nemesis. On March 19, 1995, Flair, disguised in women's clothing and a wig, attacked Savage. At Slamboree '95 in May, Flair and Hulk Hogan united to take on Flair and Big Van Vader. Angelo Poffo, Savage's father, was at ringside. When Flair, Vader, and Arn Anderson attacked Savage, Poffo climbed into the ring to help his son. Vader and Flair responded by pummeling the 70-year-old man, then Flair put him in a figure-four leglock.

Savage couldn't control his anger. "Put all three of them in a cage with me, I don't care," he said. "I don't care if I win or if I lose. This isn't about winning or losing, this is about revenge."

On November 26, 1995, Savage won his first WCW World title. A month later, on December 27, Flair beat Savage for the belt. Another month later, on January 23, Savage regained the title from Flair.

Then Elizabeth reappeared on the scene. She was in Savage's corner at SuperBrawl VI for his February 1996 match against Flair, but it was a ruse. Elizabeth handed Flair one of her high-heeled shoes, and he used it to knock out Savage and win the belt. The matches subsided, but month after month, Flair and Elizabeth continued to taunt Savage. He claimed he didn't care, but his face said otherwise.

BRET HART VS. JERRY LAWLER

The feud began on June 13, 1993, when Hart won the WWF's annual King of the Ring tournament, making him the WWF's king for a full year. The problem was, Lawler had always referred to himself as "the King." Lawler ran to the ring, claimed he was the real king, and ordered Hart to kiss his feet. Of course, Hart refused. Then Lawler struck him with a scepter and kicked Hart while he was down.

Quickly, it turned into a family feud. Eight days later, Owen Hart, Bret's younger brother, went to Memphis and won the United States Wrestling Association (USWA) heavyweight title from Papa Shango. Lawler was there that night, and Owen took the time to return the favor for his brother, thrashing Lawler.

The feud continued. At SummerSlam '93, Hart had Lawler beaten with his sharpshooter leglock, but was ruled to have used excessive force while applying the move. Lawler won by reverse decision.

Hart and Lawler's war continued until two years later at the 1995 King of the Ring pay-per-view, when Hart beat Lawler in a "kiss-my-feet match." Lawler did as he was told and kissed Bret's feet.

THE ULTIMATE WARRIOR VS. THE UNDERTAKER

Fear was The Undertaker's most dangerous weapon back in 1991. He scared the daylights out of the Ultimate Warrior, the muscular power wrestler most people assumed was scared of nobody.

The feud started when The Undertaker and his manager, Paul Bearer, locked Warrior in a casket. Several WWF officials had to rescue the Warrior, who was unconscious when they opened the box. Fortunately, WWF referee Dave Hebner knew how to perform CPR (cardio-pulmonary resuscitation), and the Warrior was saved.

As the Warrior's fear escalated, he and The Undertaker met in a series of body bag matches which The Undertaker usually won.

Finally, without warning, the Ultimate Warrior left the federation.

The feud between Undertaker and Ultimate Warrior ended when the Warrior disappeared from the WWF, leaving fans wondering if Undertaker had scared him out of the federation.

HULK HOGAN VS. SERGEANT SLAUGHTER

It was 1991, the year of the Persian Gulf War. American troops were fighting in Iraq, and Sergeant Slaughter, a former Marine drill sergeant, was suddenly parading around in a turban, waving an Iraqi flag, and screaming anti-American slogans.

Hulk Hogan, America's hero, rode to the rescue, but not before Slaughter won the WWF World title at the 1991 Royal Rumble.

This feud didn't last long, but the emotions involved were sky-high. It became the main

Larry Zbyszko, right, and Sergeant Slaughter were both involved in major feuds: Zybsko with his former mentor, Bruno Sammartino, and Slaughter with Hulk Hogan, who was incensed by Slaughter's anti-American behavior during the Persian Gulf War.

event of WrestleMania VII on March 24, 1991, in Los Angeles.

Hogan pinned Slaughter to regain the World title for America, but after the match, Slaughter refused to accept his defeat. He threw fire in Hogan's face as the Hulkster made his way back to the dressing room. The feud intensified. At SummerSlam '91, Hogan and the Ultimate Warrior teamed to humble Slaughter and his mideast friends, Colonel Mustafa and General Adnan.

Finally, Slaughter renounced his allegiance to Iraq and begged for forgiveness. Hogan, and America, were slow to forgive.

RICK RUDE VS. JAKE ROBERTS

When "Ravishing" Rick Rude flirted with the wrong woman, he ended up having to battle the wrong man—Jake "the Snake" Roberts, a wrestler famous for bringing his pet snakes to the ring and using them on his opponents.

Rude was egotistical, and considered himself to be any woman's dream man. He was absolutely convinced that every woman in the world adored him, even Mrs. Roberts. Cheryl Roberts took offense. She slapped Rude's face several times, but that didn't deter Ravishing Rick from pursuing her. He even had Cheryl's likeness airbrushed on the front of his wrestling tights. Roberts's anger grew as Rude's boldness increased. The Snake ultimately humiliated the arrogant Rude and defended his wife's honor.

RIC FLAIR VS. TERRY FUNK

The feud started at WCW's Music City Showdown pay-per-view on May 7, 1989, when Flair defeated Rick Steamboat to regain the World heavyweight title. When Funk entered the ring after the match, it looked as if he wanted to shake Flair's hand. He shook things up in a different way, brutally attacking Flair and igniting their feud.

Funk hated Flair from the bottom of his heart. Flair, on the other hand, had once had great respect for Funk, a smart, tough Texan who had remarkable courage and determination. But Funk's actions in this feud, which included trying to suffocate Flair with a plastic bag, changed Flair's opinion of the former NWA World champion. And the feud changed the fans' opinion of Flair; for the first time in many years, they cheered him.

The two stars met in the main event of the July 23, 1989, Great American Bash. Flair won a great match, but the feud continued with one exhausting match after another. Flair vs. Funk became the focal point of WCW. Finally, on November 18, 1989, Flair and Funk had a showdown in an "I Quit" match in Troy, New York. Flair won, forcing Funk to shake his hand. The feud that started with a handshake also ended with a handshake.

TAZ VS. SABU

On October 1, 1993, Taz lost to Sabu in his Extreme Championship Wrestling (ECW) debut. They were friends for a while. In 1994, Taz saved Sabu from an attack by the tag team known as the Pit Bulls. Taz and Sabu formed a team that won the ECW World tag team title. But when Sabu left for WCW, and was welcomed back to ECW with open arms, Taz was enraged. He wondered why Sabu had received preferential treatment, when he had been loyal to ECW for all these years.

Taz called for a bout with Sabu for months without any response. Finally Sabu did respond, igniting a feud that, even at the time of Taz's 1999 departure to the WWF, had not ended. Fans packed ECW's tiny arenas to watch them wage giant wars.

At ECW's first pay-per-view on April 13, 1997, Taz defeated Sabu. Afterwards, Sabu's tag team partner Rob Van Dam attacked Taz, then Van Dam and Sabu both attacked Taz. Then Bill Alfonso, Taz's manager, tore off his Team Taz shirt to reveal a Sabu T-shirt underneath. Now it was a full-scale war.

Taz pinned Sabu. Sabu pinned Taz. The feud raged on and on. They briefly reunited, then broke up again. In 1999, Taz won the ECW World title, and faced off against Sabu at the Living Dangerously pay-per-view on March 21, 1999. In this classic falls-count-anywhere match, both men used chairs and tables on each other. Finally, Taz won by submission.

There had always been deep respect between both men, but there remained something that drove each to try and destroy the other.

THE GREAT TAG TEAM FEUDS

4

A s the sport moved into the new millennium, the emphasis was on singles battles, and battles among the members of various cliques. Tag teams formed and dissolved frequently. In the 1980s and early 1990s, however, when tag teams ruled the wrestling world, several feuds electrified it.

THE FREEBIRDS VS. THE VON ERICHS

One family of sports heroes managed to capture the hearts of wrestling fans deep in the heart of Texas like no other—the Von Erichs. In the early 1980s, and especially in 1983, Kevin, Kerry, and David Von Erich were as big a trio of sports celebrities as the Lone Star state had ever known. Fresh-faced, strong, family men, the Von Erichs were the ultimate good guys. Their enemies were the ultimate bad guys—the Fabulous Freebirds, a bunch of rough-edged, tough-talking rock 'n' rollers who had no use for the pretty boys. Their names were Michael Hayes, Buddy Roberts, and Terry Gordy. In the world of Texas wrestling, no trio of men were ever more hated.

The feud started innocently enough on December 25, 1982, when Kerry Von Erich battled NWA World champion Ric Flair in

The Fabulous Freebirds pose with one of their wrestling trophies. For five years, the rulebreaking Freebirds feuded with the Von Erich brothers, packing arenas and igniting the wrath of Texas wrestling fans.

a steel cage match in Dallas. Michael Hayes served as special referee, and he was clearly on Von Erich's side. When Von Erich and Flair collided in the ring, knocking both men into near-unconsciousness, Hayes placed Von Erich on top of Flair and counted the pin.

Von Erich, a straight-and-narrow type of guy, refused to accept the title that way, which enraged Hayes. "You're an idiot!" Hayes screamed at him. As Von Erich left the cage, Hayes's partner, Gordy, who was at ringside for the bout, slammed the door on his head, igniting a war that would last for nearly five years. The Von Erichs vs. the Freebirds packed arenas.

THE MIDNIGHT EXPRESS VS. THE ROCK 'N' ROLL EXPRESS

Like the Von Erichs vs. the Freebirds, this was a classic good guys vs. bad guys feud. The good guys were the Rock 'n' Roll Express, Rick Morton and Robert Gibson. The bad guys were the Midnight Express, Dennis Condrey and Bobby Eaton, whose manager, Jim Cornette, who would stop at nothing to win. Cornette carried his tennis racket to ringside, where he often used it on the Rock 'n' Rolls.

This feud defined tag team wrestling in the mid-1980s for many wrestling fans and raged with particular intensity throughout 1986. At times, it seemed as if the Rock 'n' Rolls and the Midnights were the only tag teams in the NWA, as they met over and over again in battles.

Morton and Gibson had won the NWA World tag team belts twice in 1985, and their second reign lasted until Condrey and Eaton won the title on February 2, 1986. Six months later in Philadelphia, the Rock 'n' Rolls regained the championship. At Starrcade '87, the Rock 'n' Rolls defeated the Midnights in a terrifying match fought on a scaffold high above the ring.

Neither team won the feud. The decisive winner in this war were the fans, who were treated to some of the most incredibly fast-paced tag team bouts the sport has ever seen.

THE MEGAPOWERS VS. THE MEGABUCKS

The Megapowers were Hulk Hogan and Randy Savage, by far the two most popular men in the WWF in 1988. The Megabucks were Ted DiBiase and Andre the Giant, by far the two least popular men in wrestling at the time.

DiBiase, also known as the "Million-Dollar Man," was all about money and greed. Since he couldn't win the WWF World title on his own, he tried to buy it. He hired an impostor referee to fix a match between Hogan and Andre the Giant for the WWF World title. When Andre won the title by nefarious means, he immediately sold it to DiBiase. WWF officials nullified the deal, declared the title vacant, and put it up for grabs at WrestleMania IV. Savage and DiBiase met in the finals of the tournament, and Hogan helped Savage score a remarkable victory for the title. Hogan and Savage, former rivals, were now a team with the beautiful Elizabeth as their centerpiece.

They were only interested in revenge. The Megapowers and the Megabucks met in the main event of SummerSlam '88 at Madison Square Garden in New York. The turning point in the bout came when Elizabeth stood on a turnbuckle and dropped her skirt, revealing a skimpy bikini. That distracted the Megabucks and helped lead the Megapowers to victory.

Hart Foundation members, Bret Hart and Jim Neidhart, stand in the center of the ring before the Battle Royal at WrestleMania IV.

THE BRITISH BULLDOGS VS. THE HART FOUNDATION

The Hart Foundation—Bret Hart and Jim Neidhart—were hardworking mat wrestlers who easily could have won matches without any help. But Jimmy Hart (who was no relation to Bret) was their fast-talking, megaphone-carrying, rule-breaking manager.

It was Jimmy Hart's idea to team Bret Hart with his brother-in-law, Jim "the Anvil" Neidhart. With Jimmy leading the way with his constant interference, the Hart Foundation became one of the top tag teams in the WWF in the mid-1980s. Once together, they set their sights on the British Bulldogs, the WWF World tag team champions. They'd do anything to win, even pay off a referee.

The crooked referee was Danny Davis, who ended up with a pocketful of cash thanks to Jimmy Hart. When the Bulldogs and the Harts met on January 26, 1987, in Tampa, Florida, the Bulldogs really didn't stand a chance. Davis conveniently ignored Jimmy Hart's interference and made a fast count on the final pin attempt that made the Hart Foundation World tag team champions. The Bulldogs, incensed by Davis's actions and Hart's arrogance, desperately wanted to even the score. At WrestleMania III, the Bulldogs and Tito Santana faced off against the Hart Foundation and Davis. Late in the match, Davis grabbed Jimmy Hart's megaphone and hit Davey Boy Smith, then pinned Smith for the win.

The Bulldogs never got their revenge.

HARLEM HEAT VS. THE NASTY BOYS

The Nasty Boys might have been the most disgusting tag team in history. Jerry Sags and Brian Knobs were proud of their grossness, perfecting "maneuvers" like shoving opponents' faces into their smelly, sweaty armpits.

The red-hot war between the Nasty Boys and Harlem Heat—Booker T and Stevie Ray, accompanied by manager Sherri Martel—started in December 1994, shortly after Harlem Heat won the WCW World tag team title. At Slamboree '95 in May, Sags connected with a top-rope elbowsmash on Booker T, then scored the pin. The Nasty Boys were World tag team champions.

But Harlem Heat got their revenge in the ring by regaining the belts from the Nasty Boys in June, and going on to hold the WCW World tag team title on five more occasions. The Nastys would never regain the WCW tag team belts and soon faded from the WCW tag team scene.

Nasty Boy Jerry Sags wrestles an unlucky opponent. The Nasty Boys were known for pushing opponents' faces into their armpits.

5   THE BLOOD FEUDS

Some feuds are about pride, some are about titles, and some are about something that can't be explained, feelings that rumble deep inside a wrestler's soul, and hatreds that defy all reason and logic. These are the blood feuds.

Of course, world championships and personal pride have often been on the line in blood feuds. Yet for reasons that can't always be defined, the blood feuds are the ones that grow longer, nastier, and bloodier than the average feud between two wrestlers.

RIC FLAIR VS. DUSTY RHODES

Ric Flair, the man known as the "Nature Boy," and Dusty Rhodes, the man known as the "American Dream," were the two dominant wrestlers of the 1980s in the NWA. Although Flair was mostly hated by the fans, he parlayed his style, cockiness, and all-around wrestling ability into seven NWA World title reigns during the '80s alone.

Flair won his first NWA World title by beating Rhodes on September 17, 1981. For the next seven years, Flair vs. Rhodes was always a main event. Rhodes battled for the everyday working man, while Flair often hid behind the interference of his group, the Four Horsemen. The contrast between the two

When Jerry Lawler used his piledriver, shown here on Road Warrior Hawk, against comedian Andy Kaufman during their 1982 bout, he broke Kaufman's vertebrae.

For nearly a decade the conniving Ric Flair and Dusty Rhodes feuded in the NWA, with each man holding the championship belt more than once.

couldn't have been greater: Flair was slick, supremely confident, outrageously outspoken, and always seemed to have a beautiful woman on his arm. Rhodes was overweight, covered with scars, and loved country music.

Their feud peaked in 1986, resulting in both men gaining increased respect—and hatred—for each other. Flair had been NWA World champion for two years, two months, and two days when he stepped into the ring against Rhodes for a steel cage match on July 26, 1986, in the sold-out Greensboro, North Carolina, Coliseum. Rhodes walked out of the arena that night with the belt, and Flair went on a two-week vacation after conceding that Rhodes was the better man. In his first title defense on August 9, 1986, Flair regained the belt from Rhodes and gloated in his face. That was the last time the American Dream would be champion.

JERRY LAWLER VS. ANDY KAUFMAN

Fifty years from now, when people sit around discussing the greatest feuds in wrestling history, this is the one they are likely to name first. Certainly, it's the feud that even people who aren't wrestling fans know about, the wrestler vs. the wacky stand-up comedian. The feud put wrestling on the front pages of newspapers nationwide. The feud was even immortalized in the 1999 movie, *Man on the Moon*, the story of Kaufman's life.

Lawler vs. Kaufman started when Lawler felt the comedian was belittling the sport by challenging females to wrestling matches on television and in his nightclub act. Kaufman claimed to be the "Intergender Wrestling Champion of the World" because he was undefeated after wrestling over 200 women. Partly in defense of the sport and partly capitalizing on the opportunity to get a little publicity for himself, Lawler challenged Kaufman to a match at the Mid-South Coliseum in Memphis, Tennessee. Kaufman accepted, and the bout was set for April 5, 1982. The wrestler had no mercy on Kaufman. Lawler gave him two piledrivers, seriously injuring Kaufman's cervical vertebrae and sending Kaufman to the hospital for three days with an injured neck.

Much to Lawler's annoyance, Kaufman continued to wear a neck brace for months after the match. On July 29, 1982, Lawler and Kaufman both appeared on *Late Night with David Letterman.*

"My father said, my manager said, everyone said that I could have gone to a lawyer and I could have sued you for everything that you're worth," Kaufman told Lawler. "But I didn't. All I want is an apology."

Lawler didn't apologize. He slapped Kaufman out of his chair. Kaufman responded by shouting curses and tossing Letterman's hot coffee in Lawler's face before fleeing from the studio. The incident made headlines in newspapers across the United States. Suddenly, Lawler and Kaufman were household names. To the fans in Memphis, and to most wrestling fans worldwide, Lawler was the hero and Kaufman was the villain. Everywhere else in America, however,

Lawler was seen by the general public as a thug who couldn't take a joke.

The Letterman incident was the most famous showdown between the two, but there were others, such as when Kaufman agreed to team with Lawler, then shockingly turned against him, enraging the pro-Lawler fans in Memphis.

Kaufman died in 1984. But the feud lived on, at least in Lawler's mind. During the filming of *Man on the Moon*, Lawler was brought back to recreate the famous incident on David Letterman's show, this time with actor Jim Carrey, who portrayed Kaufman. Perhaps Carrey's portrayal of Kaufman was too realistic; Lawler slapped Carrey across the face, drawing blood from the right side of the actor's mouth. Like Kaufman, Carrey was shown on televised news reports wearing a neck brace.

BUZZ SAWYER VS. TOMMY RICH

When wrestlers get embroiled in feuds that seemingly have nothing to do with their championship aspirations, wrestlers and journalists alike are sure to warn, "Don't end up like Buzz Sawyer and Tommy Rich."

Rich and Sawyer, two tough-talking brawlers with tons of ability, didn't feud over titles, they feuded because they hated each other. By the time their war was over, they had long ago forgotten why. Indeed, this became the battle by which all others would be measured for intensity and sheer animosity.

"Wildfire" Rich, blond and immensely popular, and "Mad Dog" Sawyer, a scrappy brawler, just about destroyed each other's careers with their long and brutal war. Their matches were fought at the expense of pursuing all other career goals. At one point, the editors of a national wrestling magazine demanded that they settle their differences in a cage, just so a decisive winner could be declared. After all, Rich wasn't just another wrestler; in 1981, he had been NWA World heavyweight champion. His career held immense promise. After his feud with Sawyer, much of the promise faded. Rich would never again get close to world championship gold.

After 18 months of weekly battles, the feud finally ended on October 23, 1983, when Rich and Sawyer stepped into a steel cage. By the time the match ended, both men had blood pouring down their faces. Rich was the winner, as far as the match was concerned. However, both men lost the feud.

Sawyer died in 1992, at the age of 32. Rich's career continued, but he never regained the

Buzz "Mad Dog" Sawyer was so consumed by his feud with Tommy Rich that he had time for little else. Both men let their rivalry cause them to lose sight of larger career goals.

popularity or high profile of his early-1980s
NWA days.

RANDY SAVAGE VS. "DIAMOND" DALLAS PAGE

Randy "Macho Man" Savage and "Diamond"
Dallas Page (DDP) had both wrestled on WCW
cards for more than two years, but they rarely
crossed paths. Then, in early 1997, shortly
after Savage joined the rulebreaking clique
known as the NWO, he saw a copy of a men's
magazine featuring Kimberly Page, Dallas's
wife, in revealing photographs.

Savage gleefully displayed the pictures of
Kimberly on national television. Page was out-
raged. Savage, with his wife Elizabeth at his
side, knew he had gotten Page's attention, and
he wouldn't relent. At WCW's Uncensored '97
pay-per-view event, Savage and Elizabeth
unleashed a humiliating attack on Kimberly,
spray-painting her entire body.

Savage and Page squared off at the April 6,
1997, Spring Stampede pay-per-view card in
what turned out to be one of the most intense,
all-out brawls of the year. Page, inspired by his
hatred for Savage and his desire to avenge the
honor of his wife, unleashed a brutal attack
and pinned the Macho Man. To Page, it was one
of the defining moments of his career.

"When that ref slapped his hand down for
the three-count, I knew that I had arrived,"
Page said afterward, "but all I could think
about was how much I hated Savage and how
I wanted to tear into him even more."

He got his chance for a win at the Great
American Bash two months later. However,
Savage pinned Page thanks to the interference
of Scott Hall, his buddy from the NWO. The

feud continued over the next four months with matches throughout the United States. Savage and Page both had victories, with neither man gaining a clear advantage in the feud.

"What scares me is that they'll get to Kimberly sometime when I'm not around," Page told one national wrestling magazine. "That thought scares me, because I didn't want her dragged into this."

He had no choice. At WCW's Halloween Havoc pay-per-view card on October 26, 1997, Page and Savage squared off in a death match. This time, Elizabeth interfered on Savage's behalf, and Page lost again.

As far as the fans were concerned, however, Savage was among the most hated men in wrestling, while Page was one of the most popular. Although he lost twice to Savage at pay-per-view events, DDP's career was revitalized by his feud with Savage.

FEUDS OF THE '90s

A t the start of the new millennium, pro wrestling had become hotter than ever and one of the most popular sports in the world. WCW's *Nitro* and the WWF's *Raw* were two of the highest-rated programs on cable television. Wrestlers graced the covers of national magazines, ranging from *TV Guide* to *U.S. News and World Report*. One former wrestler, Jesse Ventura, was elected governor of Minnesota. Wrestling had joined the mainstream.

Two feuds were responsible for taking wrestling from a sport with a cult-like following to one viewed by tens of millions of fans each week.

THE NWO VS. WCW

On February 19, 1996, the WWF suspended Razor Ramon for six weeks due to what the federation deemed "unprofessional conduct." On March 5, 1996, the WWF announced that Diesel would be leaving the federation to compete in WCW. At the time, nobody could have guessed what kind of impact these two moves would have on the sport of wrestling.

In early 1996, WCW was clearly the number-two federation in North America, trailing the WWF, which had been on top of the wrestling world since Hulk Hogan ruled the sport in

---

Friends Razor Ramon and Diesel decided to use their real names of Scott Hall and Kevin Nash when they stormed the halls of WCW in 1996, forming the Outsiders, a clique that later become known as the NWO.

the mid-1980s. All that was about to change. On May 27, 1996, Ramon, using his real name of Scott Hall, emerged from the audience at *Nitro* and announced that he was rounding up all of his old friends from the WWF to declare war on WCW. "You'll know who my friends are when I want you to know," was Hall's cocky statement.

The world found out soon enough. On June 10, Diesel, using his real name of Kevin Nash, joined Hall and declared himself the second of three men in a group known as the Outsiders. At the Great American Bash pay-per-view card on June 16, WCW executive Eric Bischoff asked Nash and Hall if they still worked for the WWF. Nash and Hall told him that they didn't. When Bischoff refused to tell them who they'd be facing at the next pay-per-view event, Hall punched him in the stomach and Nash power-bombed him through the stage.

Much to everyone's surprise, the third Outsider was Hulk Hogan, who had been a fan favorite for well over a decade, and was perhaps the most popular wrestler in history.

"It's time for Hulk Hogan to look out for Hulk Hogan, brother," Hogan said as fans pelted the ring with garbage and soft drinks. "I've been standin' up for these people for a lot of years, and what thanks do I get? Nothing! Those people can stick it! They don't mean anything to me!"

The Outsiders's simple goal was to take over WCW and win every major title. From that point on, the Outsiders would be known by another name: the New World Order (NWO).

The wrestling world was shocked. Hogan a bad guy? How could it be? And how could WCW allow three men from the WWF to charge in and

When the NWO split into two factions in 1997, "Hollywood" Hogan headed the one known as NWO Hollywood.

take control of the federation? The answer was that they couldn't, and they wouldn't.

WCW wrestlers joined forces. As the NWO ran wild throughout WCW, manager Jimmy Hart recruited WCW stars—rulebreakers and fan favorites alike—to battle the NWO. Ric Flair, Steve McMichael, Lex Luger, Sting, Arn Anderson—wrestlers who had always been enemies were suddenly allies in this fight against Hall, Nash, and Hogan.

Lex Luger, Sting, Kevin Nash, and Konnan pose for an NWO Wolfpac portrait. The Wolfpac, which also included "Macho Man" Randy Savage, was NWO Hollywood's chief rival.

The NWO got stronger. Hogan got help from Nash and Hall to beat The Giant for the WCW World heavyweight title. After the match, Hogan and his NWO buddies beat up Brutus Beefcake, Hogan's former best friend. On August 20, 1996, interference by Hall and Nash caused Luger to lose the WCW TV belt. The NWO members cackled with laughter. Then, The Giant shocked the world by joining the NWO, just 23 days after he had lost the World title to Hogan.

Defections to the NWO continued. Former WWF wrestler Ted DiBiase declared himself to be the money man behind the group. Referee Nick Patrick and wrestler Syxx, later known as X-Pac in the WWF, also joined the NWO.

For the first time, WCW's *Nitro* was beating the WWF's *Raw* in the Monday-night television ratings war. All eyes were on WCW and its feud with the NWO.

The NWO was always up to no good. It even had an impostor Sting attack Luger and drive off in a limousine with other NWO members.

Later, Sting claimed he had no allegiance to either WCW or the NWO.

"Whose side are you on?" became the NWO's litmus test. If you were against them, you were targeted for annihilation.

The brutality continued. Flair was attacked by the NWO, aggravating a shoulder injury and putting him out of action for several months. Hall and Nash attacked Booker T and Stevie Ray with a cane, taking their WCW World tag team title in the bargain. Bischoff, the senior vice president of WCW, revealed his allegiance to the NWO. That night, the NWO also attacked Roddy Piper.

The drama increased. A week after joining the NWO, Bischoff announced that all WCW wrestlers had 30 days to convert their WCW contracts to NWO contracts, or they would become targets of the NWO. In January 1997, the NWO branched out and promoted its first pay-per-view event, Souled Out. The NWO was becoming a federation that was within a federation. Longtime WCW fan favorite Marcus Alexander Bagwell joined the NWO. Randy Savage joined the NWO. Sting pretended he was going to join the NWO, then attacked Hall, Nash, Savage, and Hogan at Uncensored '97.

The NWO vs. WCW was big news. Basketball megastar Dennis Rodman joined Hogan for a tag team match against Luger and The Giant, who had been kicked out of the NWO. WCW dominated the WWF in the Monday-night ratings. Wrestling fans everywhere were wearing NWO T-shirts.

Just when it appeared as if the NWO would take total control of WCW, the clique fell apart. By late 1997, Nash decided that he was sick of Hogan, who had become the group's leader. The

NWO split into two factions. Nash, along with Konnan, Savage, Sting, and Luger, formed NWO Wolfpac. The remaining members of the NWO, along with Hogan and Bischoff, formed NWO Hollywood.

Wolfpac vs. Hollywood captured the fans' imaginations, too, but not like NWO vs. WCW had. The NWO vs. WCW war had changed the sport by capturing the attention of the world.

STEVE AUSTIN VS. VINCE McMAHON

"Stone Cold" Steve Austin should have been able to celebrate when he won the WWF Intercontinental title from Owen Hart at SummerSlam '97. Unfortunately, Austin was in no physical condition to celebrate. During the match, Hart had driven his neck into the mat, and the prognosis wasn't good. Austin had a serious back injury that could result in paralysis.

Austin, however, didn't care about his injury. He didn't care about his own health. All he cared about was his career, which he felt was about to take off. He begged the WWF to let him wrestle. When federation head Vince McMahon urged him to be patient, Austin used his "Stone Cold stunner," a variation of the "bulldog" in which Austin wraps his arms around an opponent's head and drives it into the canvas, on McMahon.

Austin did return to the ring after agreeing to accept liability for any injury he suffered, and McMahon kept a close eye on him. McMahon berated Austin for driving his truck to the ring for an Intercontinental title defense against Rocky Maivia. When McMahon ordered him to defend the title again against Maivia, Austin refused and tossed the Intercontinental title belt into an adjacent river. McMahon made Maivia the new champion.

For years, thanks to the power of the NWO, WCW had been winning the Monday-night television battle over the WWF. All that was about to change. Austin, who in the past would have been booed for assaulting a federation head and disparaging a championship belt, was being cheered by the fans. Meanwhile McMahon, who in the past would have been cheered for taking on the so-called rulebreaker, was being booed. To the fans, Austin was a working-class hero, the man who had the guts to tell his boss, "Take this job and shove it!"

Austin beat up referees. He cursed. He broke the rules. He didn't care what anybody thought of him. It all made him the most popular wrestler in the world. This alarmed McMahon. A few days before Austin was scheduled to square off against World champion Shawn Michaels at WrestleMania X on March 29, 1998, McMahon publicly said that Austin as World champion would be "a public relations and promotional nightmare," for the WWF. This was an unprecedented statement. The head of the federation was actually coming out against one man in a major title bout. He was saying that Steve Austin was not the type of champion the WWF wanted.

Of course, this only made Austin even more eager to win the World title, which he did. At WrestleMania X, Austin won his first WWF World title by pinning Michaels. McMahon couldn't have been angrier, so he decided to do something about it. McMahon vowed to mold Austin into the type of champion that the federation could be proud of, the ideal corporate champion, as fan favorites Bruno Sammartino, Bob Backlund, and Hulk Hogan had been in the past. No way, said Austin, he wasn't going to be molded into anything. He hated McMahon, and he was making sure everybody else hated him as well.

"Nobody can stand that piece of trash because he's a liar, a cheat, and even worse, a yell[ow] coward," Austin said of McMahon. "All this garbage started because Vince was trying to load the deck all the time for his so-called superstars, like Bret Hart and Shawn Michaels. Vince knew what he was doin'. It was a conspiracy if I ever saw one, but it ain't gonna work when he's dealin' with 'Stone Cold,' and that's the bottom line."

Austin was absolutely correct. It didn't work with him, and it didn't work with the fans. Austin T-shirts became the hottest-selling merchandise in wrestling. Anything with Austin's name or likeness on it was a huge seller. And thanks to the feud between Austin and McMahon, the WWF's *Raw* was suddenly beating WCW in the Monday-night ratings battle for the first time since 1996.

McMahon continued to do everything in his power to get the belt away from Austin, even assigning himself as the referee for Austin's title match against Hunter Hearst Helmsley, and later against Dude Love. He assigned his corporate stooges, Pat Patterson and Jerry Brisco, as officials for matches, and forced Austin to defend his title in three-way matches against Kane and The Undertaker. The only stipulation was that Kane and Undertaker could only pin Austin, not each other.

As Austin's title reign continued throughout 1998, his popularity grew, and the WWF went along for the ride. Stone Cold was a guest on national TV shows, such as *Live with Regis and Kathie Lee* and the CBS series *Nash Bridges*. His picture was on the cover of *TV Guide*. A major article about Austin appeared in *Rolling Stone*. People who had never before watched wrestling were mesmerized by Austin vs. McMahon. When McMahon declared, "I guarantee you Steve Austin will no longer be WWF World champion after September 27, 1998," people had to tune in to see what tricks McMahon had up his sleeve.

On that date, at the WWF's Break Down pay-per-view card, Austin was forced to wrestle Kane and The Undertaker in another three-way match. This time, however, Austin couldn't overcome the odds, and he lost when Kane and Undertaker simultaneously pinned him.

During his power struggle with Vince McMahon, WWF champion Steve Austin was frequently pitted against Kane, The Undertaker's half brother.

"Give me the belt! Give me the belt!" McMahon shouted ecstatically as he ran to the ring. He got away before Austin could get his hands on him.

Of course, now there was a problem: Kane and Undertaker had pinned Austin at the same time. There couldn't be two world champions. McMahon's solution was devious and cruel: he ordered Austin to referee a match a month later between Kane and The Undertaker. "And if you don't make a three-count and raise one of their hands as champion, I will fire you," McMahon declared. Austin made two three-counts, one on Kane and one on The Undertaker, then declared himself the new champion.

That didn't cut it with McMahon, who immediately fired Austin, only to have his son, Shane McMahon, use his own power as a WWF executive to reinstate Austin. In the second round of the World title tournament at the November 15, 1998, Survivor Series, special referee Shane refused to count Austin's pin of Mankind, who went on to win the match and lose to Rocky Maivia in the championship final. Austin vs. McMahon was named Feud of the Year for 1998 by the readers of *Pro Wrestling Illustrated* magazine, but by no means did the feud end in 1998.

Insult followed insult as Vince McMahon's plottings continued. Previously, he simply hadn't wanted Austin as world champion. Now he didn't want Austin in the WWF at all. He wanted to destroy him, so he let his emotions get the better of his judgment. On February 14, 1999, at the St. Valentine's Day Massacre pay-per-view, McMahon unwisely stepped into a ring surrounded by a steel cage for a match against Austin. Austin physically destroyed McMahon.

He pushed him off the cage and sent him crashing through the broadcaster's table. When medical personnel tried to take McMahon away on a stretcher, Austin slammed it into the cage and continued his brutal attack.

The crowd cheered. When Austin dispatched Paul Wight, who tore through the bottom of the cage, to go after McMahon, another of Vince's plans was foiled. McMahon was carried back to the dressing room on a stretcher.

At WrestleMania XV on March 28, 1999, McMahon had his heart set on refereeing the match between Austin and Rocky Maivia and making sure the Rock won. WWF commissioner Shawn Michaels wouldn't allow it, however, and Austin won the match. Austin also beat The Undertaker in a match with the stipulation that if Austin won, McMahon would no longer have a prominent televised role on *Raw*.

"There was no way I wasn't walking out of the arena as the WWF champion," Austin said. "Plus, I got to put an end to the tyranny of Vince McMahon. Can you imagine not being able to appear on your own TV show?"

Of course, McMahon continued to appear on *Raw*, sometimes as a wrestler, and Austin continued to get in his face. The Austin vs. McMahon feud settled down a bit in 1999, but its embers continued to burn. Stone Cold faced several months away from the ring in early 2000 after much-needed neck surgery.

Meanwhile, the WWF remained so popular, it decided to issue stock and become a public company. Now wrestling fans could own a piece of the action they loved to watch and the wrestlers they both cheered and booed.

Chronology

1959 "Cowboy" Bob Ellis and the Bruiser start their long feud when Bruiser makes disparaging remarks about the way Ellis dresses

1964 The feud between Edouard Carpentier and Killer Kowalski becomes the hottest in pro wrestling

1974 A match between Jack Brisco and Dory Funk is called "the greatest match in 30 years" by *The Wrestler* magazine

1980 The feud between Bruno Sammartino and former partner Larry Zbyszko culminates in front of a record crowd at Shea Stadium in New York when Sammartino beats Zbyszko in a cage match

1982 Michael Hayes's interference in a match between Kerry Von Erich and Ric Flair ignites the most famous feud in Texas wrestling history: the Von Erichs vs. the Freebirds; comedian Andy Kaufman feuds with wrestler Jerry Lawler, who breaks Kaufman's neck, drawing national attention to the feud

1986 A feud between Hulk Hogan and Paul Orndorff is ignited when Hogan refuses to take Orndorff's phone call during a training session

1987 A record crowd of 93,173 fans watches Hulk Hogan pin Andre the Giant at WrestleMania III in Pontiac, Michigan; the feud between Randy Savage and Rick Steamboat reaches its peak when Steamboat pins Savage for the WWF Intercontinental title

1988 Randy Savage and Hulk Hogan—the Megapowers—feud with Ted DiBiase and Andre the Giant—the Megabucks

1989 The Megapowers break up and feud over Elizabeth; a feud between WCW World champion Ric Flair and all-time great Terry Funk captures the wrestling world's imagination

1993 A heartbreaking feud between the Hart brothers, Bret and Owen, begins when Owen attacks his brother at the Survivor Series

1996 The NWO is formed and tries to take control of WCW

1997 The face of wrestling changes as fans side with Steve Austin, the apparent rulebreaker, in a feud against Bret Hart; Taz and Sabu, former tag team partners, intensify their feud in ECW

1998 Steve Austin wins the WWF World heavyweight title at WrestleMania XIV, enraging WWF head Vince McMahon; their feud makes the WWF the most popular federation in North America

1999 The war between Ric Flair and Hulk Hogan reaches a new level as Flair defeats Hogan for the WCW World heavyweight title—his fifth—at the Uncensored pay-per-view card

Further Reading

Burkett, Harry. "Bret Hart & DDP: Will Work for Feud!" *The Wrestler* (April 1999): 42–45.

Burkett, Harry. "Undertaker vs. Austin: Our Five-Point Plan to End This Feud Forever!" *Inside Wrestling* (November 1999): 38–41.

Burkett, Harry. "The WCW-NWO War! 10 Crucial Factors That Will Decide the Winner!" *Wrestle America* (June 1999): 22–25.

Hunter, Matt. *The Story of the Wrestler They Call "Hollywood" Hulk Hogan.* Philadelphia: Chelsea House Publishers, 2000.

"Match by Match: How Starrcade '97 Reshaped the NWO vs. WCW War" *Pro Wrestling Illustrated* (May 1998): 28–31.

Mudge, Jacqueline. *Bret Hart: The Story of the Wrestler They Call "The Hitman."* Philadelphia: Chelsea House Publishers, 2000.

Mudge, Jacqueline. *Randy Savage: The Story of the Wrestler They Call "The Macho Man."* Philadelphia: Chelsea House Publishers, 2000.

Rosenbaum, Dave. "The Handshake That Shook Up ECW: the Last Thing the Taz-Sabu Feud Needs Is Respect." *Pro Wrestling Illustrated* (September 1999): 32-34, 57.

Index

Photo Credits

All-Star Sports: p. 52; Associated Press/Wide World Photos: pp. 12, 14, 15, 16; Jeff Eisenberg Sports Photography: pp. 9, 10, 18, 21, 24, 29, 38, 39, 48; David Fitzgerald: pp. 30, 34, 40, 42, 45; Sports Action: pp. 2, 6, 51, 57, 60.

DAN ROSS has spent the last 10 years observing and writing about professional wrestling. His writing on wrestling, basketball, and baseball has appeared in numerous publications around the world, and he is a frequent guest whenever European radio and television stations require an American viewpoint on wrestling. He lives in upstate New York with his wife, son, and dog, and likes to brag to neighbors about the wrestling ring in his basement. His previously published volumes on the mat sport include *The Story of the Wrestler They Call "The Undertaker"* and *Steve Austin: The Story of the Wrestler They Call "Stone Cold."*